WHO'S SICK!

WHO'S SICK!

W. B. PARK

Houghton Mifflin Company   Boston   1983

Library of Congress Cataloging in Publication Data

Park, W. B.
  Who's sick!

  Summary: Walter and Wendell both wake up very sick
on the day they think they have to go to the dentist.
  I. Title.
PZ7.P22145Wh   1983   [E]   83-8429
ISBN 0-395-33229-X

Printed in the United States of America

Y 10 9 8 7 6 5 4 3 2 1

To Evie, Bryan, Chris, Anne-Marie,
Larry, and Charlotte Web.

It was Saturday morning. Walter and Wendell
woke at exactly the same time.
"Are you (*yawn*) awake?" said Walter.

"Yes (*yawn*)," said Wendell. "I woke just before you did."

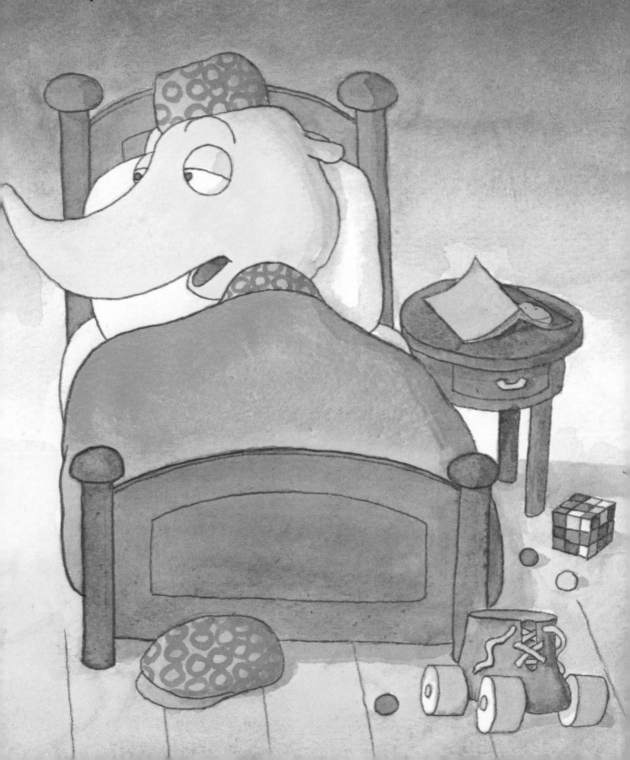

"Ha," said Walter. "I've been awake since dawn."

"I've been awake all night," said Wendell.

"Fibber!" yelled Walter.

"Storyteller!" shouted Wendell.

"Children, stop that fussing and get dressed,"
Mother called. "Today's the day."
"Today is *what* day?" wondered Walter.

"Could it be the day we go to the dentist?"
asked Wendell.

"Ohhhh," groaned Walter. "Just thinking about the dentist makes me sick."

"I'm getting a sore throat," moaned Wendell.

"I'm sicker than you," said Walter.

"No you're not," said Wendell.

"Yeah?" said Walter. "Listen to this:
Honk-sniff, honk-sniff,
honk-sniff, BLAAAAT!"

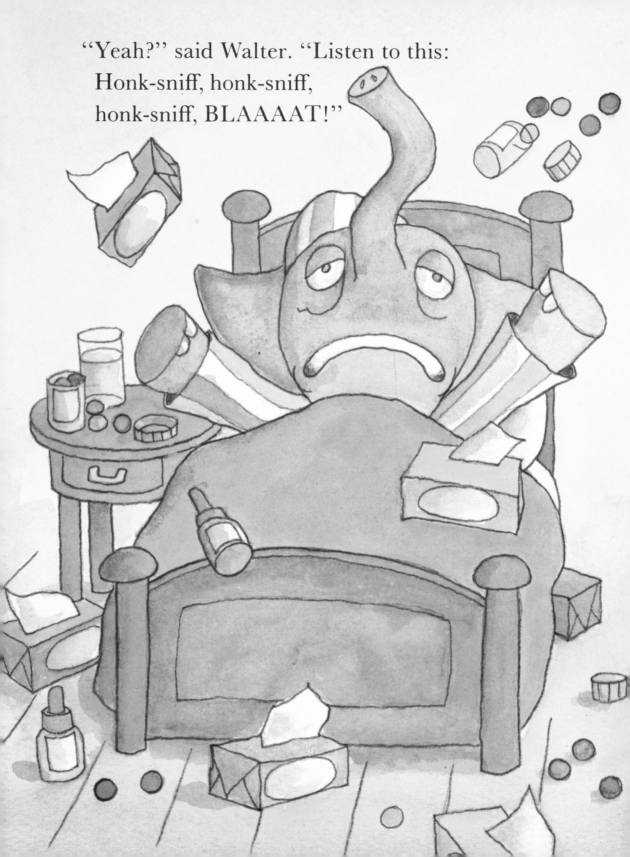

"You think that's something?" said Wendell.
"AAAAAA-hem! Cough, cough, cough,
   HAAAAAAAAAK!"

"I'm the sickest!" shouted Walter.

"No you're not. I am!" yelled Wendell.

Just then Mother came in. She was very angry.
"If this room isn't clean in five minutes," she said,
"neither of you will go on the picnic today."

Walter and Wendell looked at each other.
"Oh!" said Walter. "Today is *that* day!"

"Suddenly I feel okay," said Wendell.

"I'm sure I feel better than you do," said Walter.

"Yeah?" said Wendell. "Watch how fast I clean this room."

The beach was bright and sunny.
"Bet I have more fun than you," said Walter.
"Yeah?" said Wendell. "Just you wait and see."